UP GOES THE
SKYSCRAPER

New and Updated

BY GAIL GIBBONS

HOLIDAY HOUSE • NEW YORK

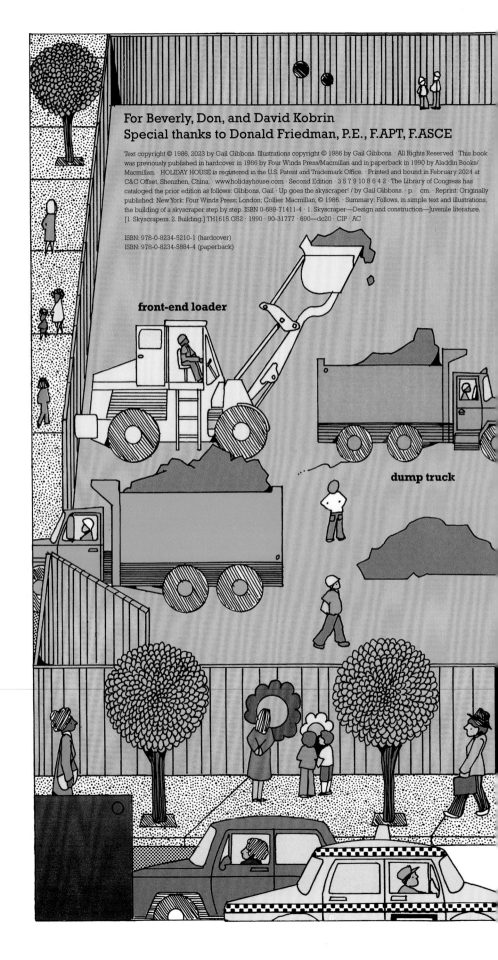

For Beverly, Don, and David Kobrin
Special thanks to Donald Friedman, P.E., F.APT, F.ASCE

Text copyright © 1986, 2023 by Gail Gibbons. Illustrations copyright © 1986 by Gail Gibbons. · All Rights Reserved · This book was previously published in hardcover in 1986 by Four Winds Press/Macmillan and in paperback in 1990 by Aladdin Books/ Macmillan. · HOLIDAY HOUSE is registered in the U.S. Patent and Trademark Office. · Printed and bound in February 2024 at C&C Offset, Shenzhen, China. · www.holidayhouse.com · Second Edition · 3 5 7 9 10 8 6 4 2 · The Library of Congress has cataloged the prior edition as follows: Gibbons, Gail · Up goes the skyscraper! / by Gail Gibbons. · p.   cm. · Reprint: Originally published: New York: Four Winds Press; London; Collier Macmillan, © 1986. · Summary: Follows, in simple text and illustrations, the building of a skyscraper step by step. ISBN 0-689-71411-4 · 1. Skyscraper—Design and construction—Juvenile literature. · [1. Skyscrapers. 2. Building.] TH1615.G52 · 1990 · 90-31777 · 690—dc20 · CIP · AC

ISBN: 978-0-8234-5210-1 (hardcover)
ISBN: 978-0-8234-5884-4 (paperback)

front-end loader

dump truck

backhoe

Thousands of people want to work and live on the empty city block. It is a small space for so many people. A skyscraper must be built.

A **core sample** is taken to see what is underneath the soil. This tells the builders what kind of foundation to build.

The **owner** will pay for the construction of the skyscraper.

The **city inspector** gives the owner a **building permit**, or permission to build.

Surveyors measure where the foundation will be.

First, a site survey is done to study the ground for the *foundation*, the part of the skyscraper below the ground.

The **foundation engineer** designs the foundation.

The weight of the building is figured out by the **structural engineer**.

Many people use computers, and some people draft by hand, too. Plans for the foundation...

Architects design the skyscraper.

and for the rest of the skyscraper are made.

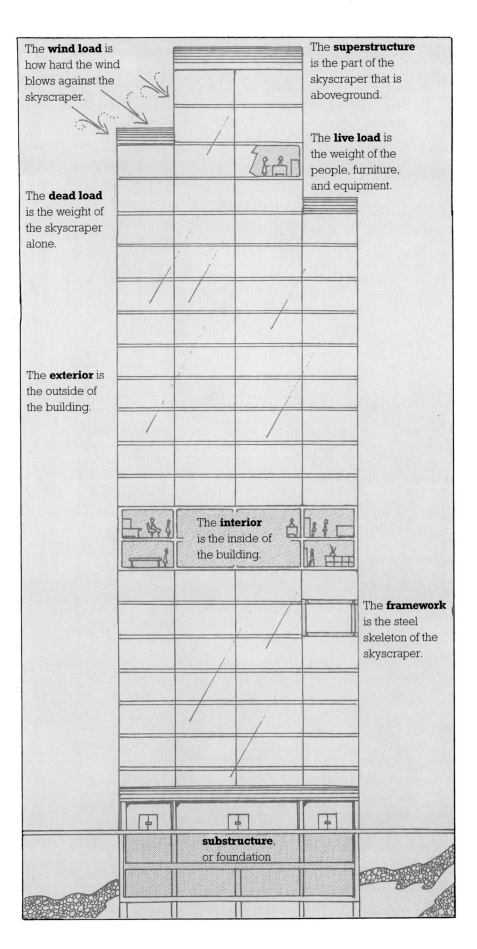

The **wind load** is how hard the wind blows against the skyscraper.

The **superstructure** is the part of the skyscraper that is aboveground.

The **live load** is the weight of the people, furniture, and equipment.

The **dead load** is the weight of the skyscraper alone.

The **exterior** is the outside of the building.

The **interior** is the inside of the building.

The **framework** is the steel skeleton of the skyscraper.

substructure, or foundation

portable toilet

The **general contractor** schedules delivery of all equipment, workers, and supplies to the site.

After many months of planning, construction begins. The hole for the foundation is dug. It becomes deeper...

Pile drivers force the piles into the ground.

construction workers

Piles are large pillars of steel.

Bedrock is the solid layer of rock under the ground.

and deeper. For this building, piles are driven into the ground until they hit bedrock.

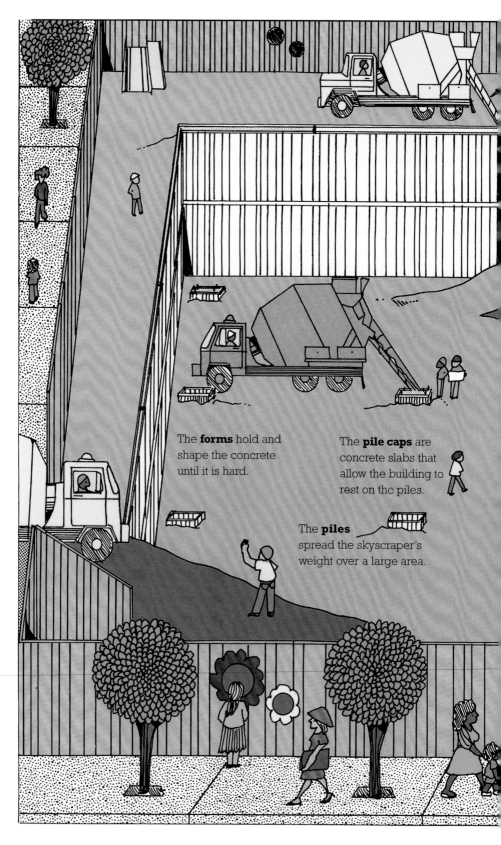

The **forms** hold and shape the concrete until it is hard.

The **pile caps** are concrete slabs that allow the building to rest on the piles.

The **piles** spread the skyscraper's weight over a large area.

Concrete is poured into wooden forms that have been placed on top of each pile to make pile caps. Metal rods stick out from each pile cap.

concrete mix truck

The **foundation walls** will be the skyscraper's basement walls.

At the same time, forms for the outer foundation wall are built. Concrete mix trucks come day and night to fill the forms.

Wooden forms are taken away...

Anchor bolts will be used to bolt tall steel columns to the pile caps.

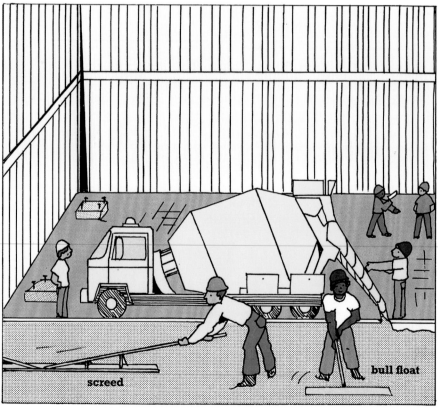

screed

bull float

When the concrete in the pile caps is hard, anchor bolts are connected to the metal rods. The concrete floor of the basement is poured and smoothed over.

The **columns**, also called **H beams**, are steel beams in the shape of an H.

once the concrete hardens.

Cranes arrive at the scene to swing columns into position. Then, the columns are bolted to the pile caps. This is the beginning of the framework.

The **floorbeams (girders)** are in the shape of an I.

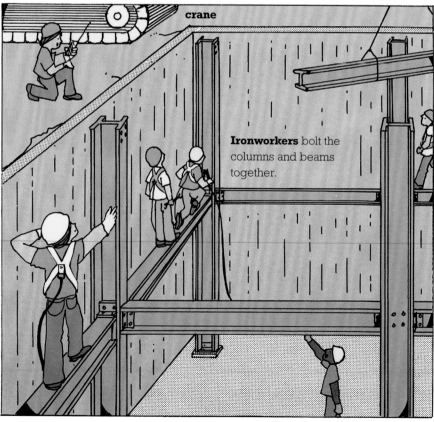

crane

Ironworkers bolt the columns and beams together.

When the columns are in place, they are connected by floorbeams.

The framework is shaped like a box. Metal decking is welded to the top of the framework. Wire mesh is placed on top of the decking and concrete is poured. This becomes the ceiling of one level and the floor of the one above it.

The **core** is made up of strong beams. It is the main support against wind and earthquakes.

crane

The same thing is done again. Now the substructure is at ground level. In the center, a core is begun. It is the strongest part of the skyscraper—the skyscraper's backbone.

Each day, the general contractor has scheduled what materials will be needed. Trucks arrive. The ironworkers add another floor...

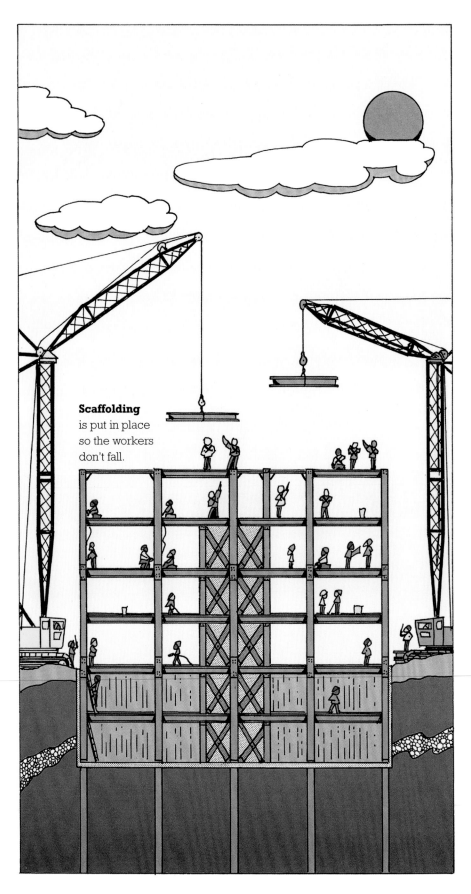

Scaffolding is put in place so the workers don't fall.

and another...

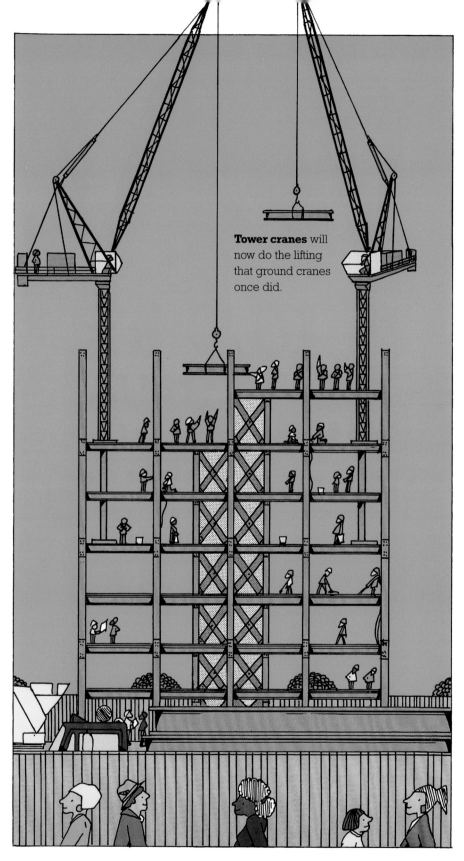

Tower cranes will now do the lifting that ground cranes once did.

and another. Tower cranes are put into place. Each floor connects into the core. The tower cranes are raised each time two levels are completed.

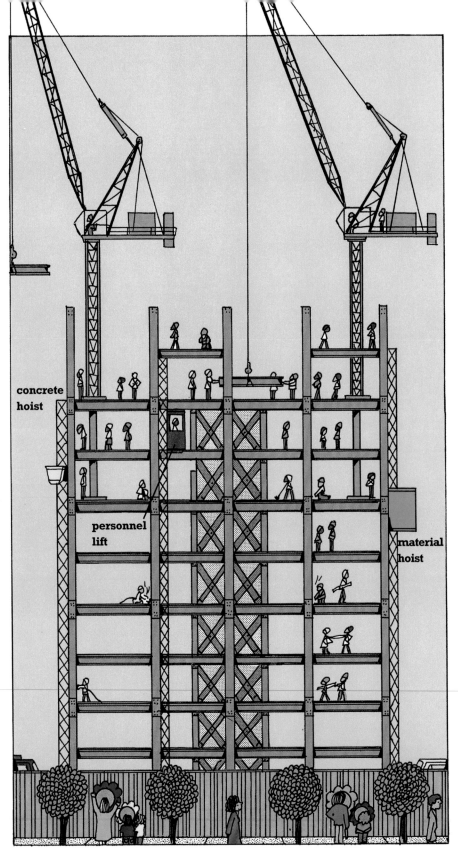

concrete hoist

personnel lift

material hoist

Up goes the skyscraper! People stop to watch. Workers go up and down on a personnel lift. Hoists are added to bring up concrete and materials.

hose used to spray fireproofing

While the ironworkers are building above, other workers are fireproofing the beams below.

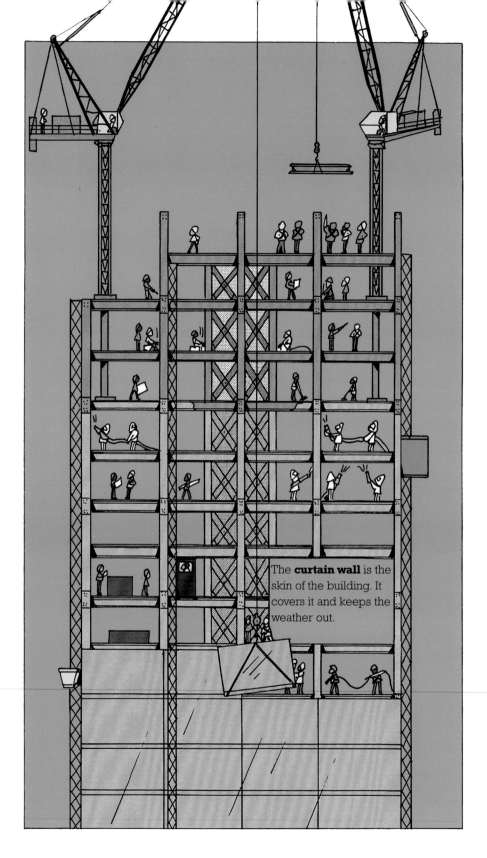

The **curtain wall** is the skin of the building. It covers it and keeps the weather out.

The tower cranes go up again. More beams are bolted into place. Below, where the fireproofing has been done, the curtain wall and windows are installed.

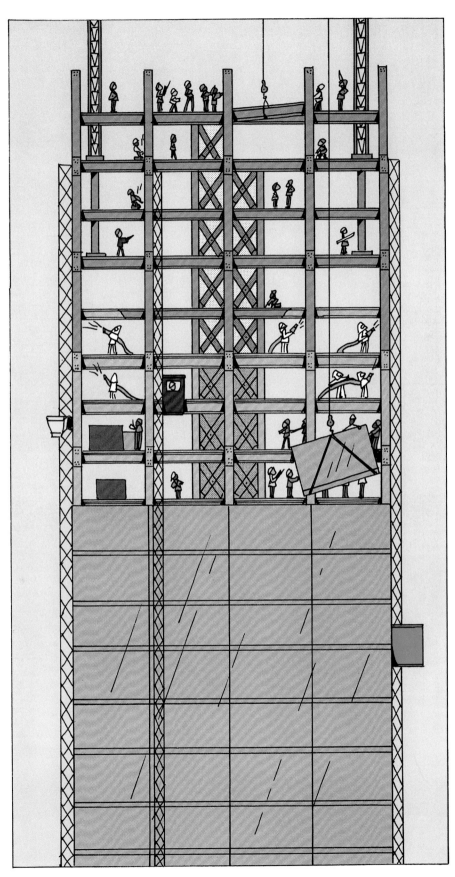

More floors are added.

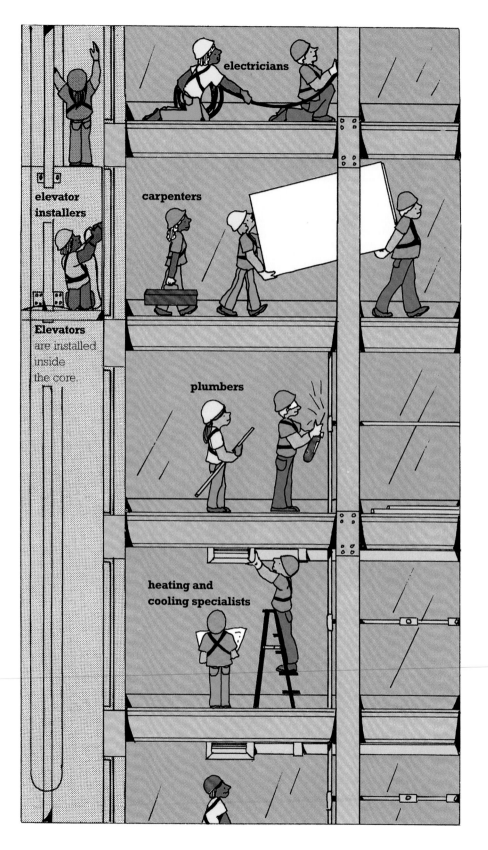

Finish workers—carpenters, plumbers, electricians, elevator installers, and heating and cooling specialists—are working below. Interior walls are added to the superstructure.

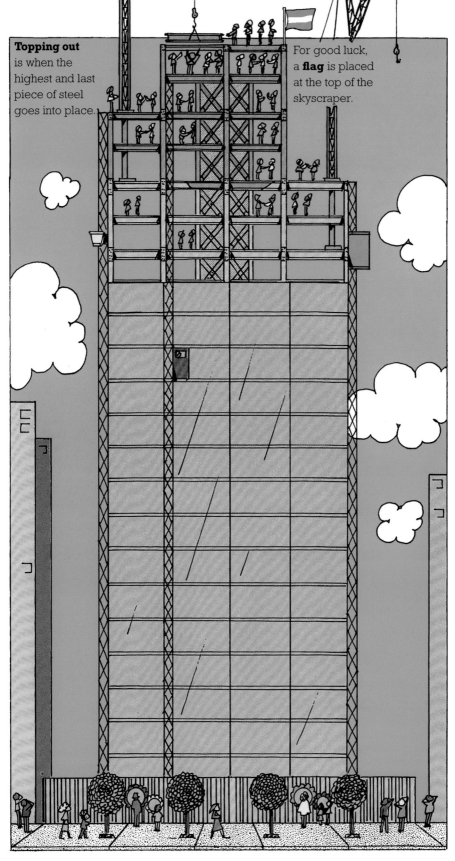

Topping out is when the highest and last piece of steel goes into place.

For good luck, a **flag** is placed at the top of the skyscraper.

The ironworkers complete the last level. The last beam swings into place. Since it is last, it is very special. The workers celebrate the topping out.

The finish workers keep on working...

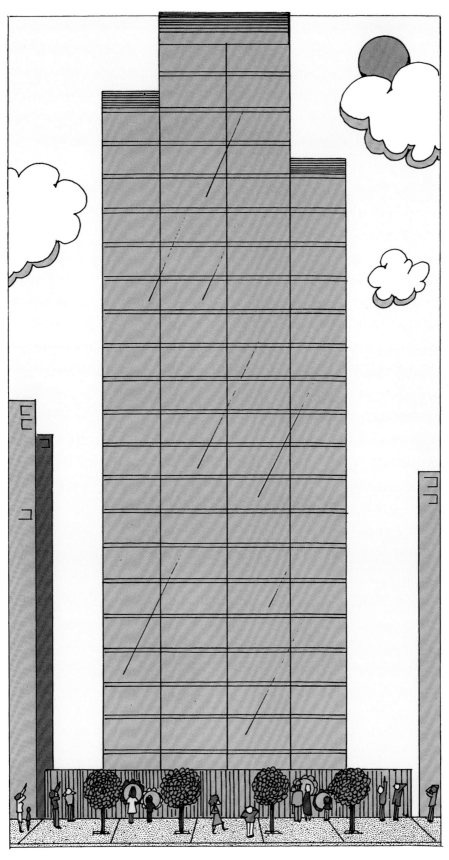

until the skyscraper is finally finished from the
bottom to the top.

Interior architects decide what the interior should look like.

telephone installers

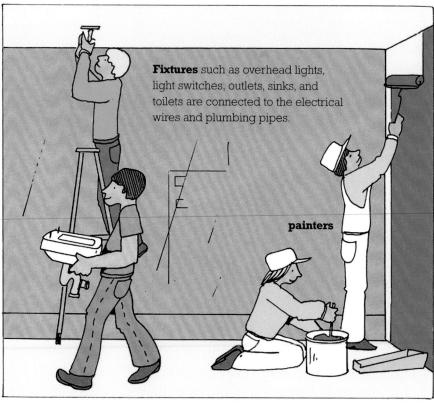

Fixtures such as overhead lights, light switches, outlets, sinks, and toilets are connected to the electrical wires and plumbing pipes.

painters

Next, the interior is designed. Fixtures and telephones are installed and sprinkler systems are added for fire safety.

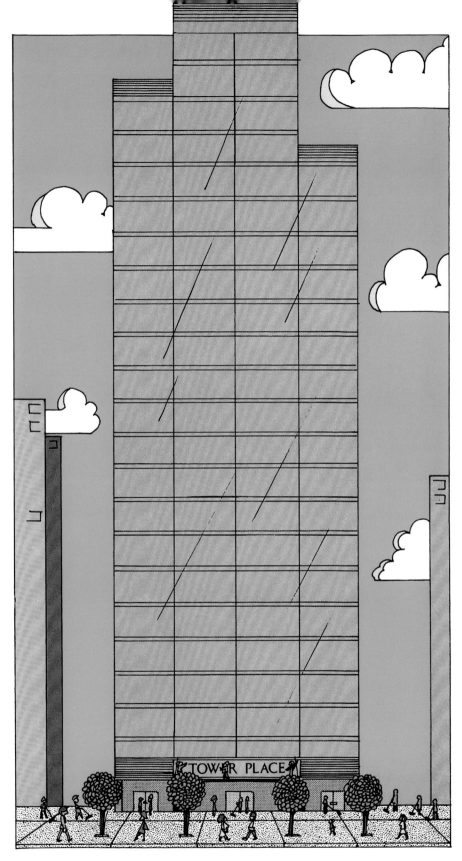

The old wooden wall with its peepholes is torn down. The area around the skyscraper is tidied up. A plaque with the skyscraper's name is put into place.

For many months, people have been watching the construction. Some have decided to rent space in the skyscraper for their businesses and homes.

Tenants are moving into the shiny new building.

Look up at the skyscraper. It took about two years to build and three hundred people to build it . . . and it is beautiful.